Seeds

Lynn Stone

Rourke

Publishing LLC

Vero Beach, Florida 32964

www.rourkepublishing.com

PHOTO CREDITS: All photos © Lynn Stone, except title pg. © Gergana Todorchovska; pg. 4 © Eric Lsselée; pg. 8 © Ljupco; pg. 8 © Ivan Josiforic; pg. 10, 15 © Malcolm Romain; pg. 12 © Jasenka Luksa; pg. 17 © Clint Scholz; pg. 20 © Alke Holwerda

Editor: Robert Stengard-Olliges

Cover design by: Nicola Stratford, bdpublishing.com

Library of Congress Cataloging-in-Publication Data

Stone, Lynn M.
  Seeds / Lynn Stone.
      p. cm. -- (Plant parts)
  ISBN 978-1-60044-555-2 (Hardcover)
  ISBN 978-1-60044-695-5 (Softcover)
  1. Seeds--Juvenile literature. I. Title.
  QK661.S76 2008
  581.4'67--dc22

                              2007015158

Printed in the USA

CG/CG

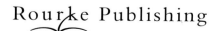

Rourke Publishing

www.rourkepublishing.com – rourke@rourkepublishing.com
Post Office Box 3328, Vero Beach, FL 32964

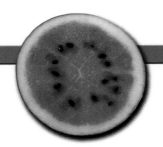

Table of Contents

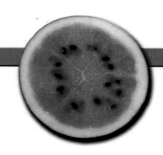

Large and Small Seeds

Seeds can be large or small. The largest seed is a kind of **coconut**. It may weigh more than 40 pounds (18 kilograms).

Bulldogs can weigh 40 pounds.

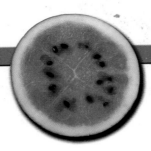

Orchids make the smallest seeds. Orchid seeds look like specks of dust. It would take almost 500 million orchid seeds to weigh one pound (500 grams)!

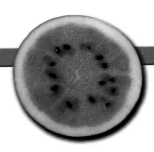

Seeds are protected by an outer cover. It may be thin or thick, hard or soft. A walnut seed is protected by a hard outer layer. Orange seeds are protected by a soft, juicy **fruit**.

Walnut Seed

Orange Seed

A New Plant

Seeds are different in many ways. But in one way, seeds are alike. Inside any seed are the beginnings of a new plant.

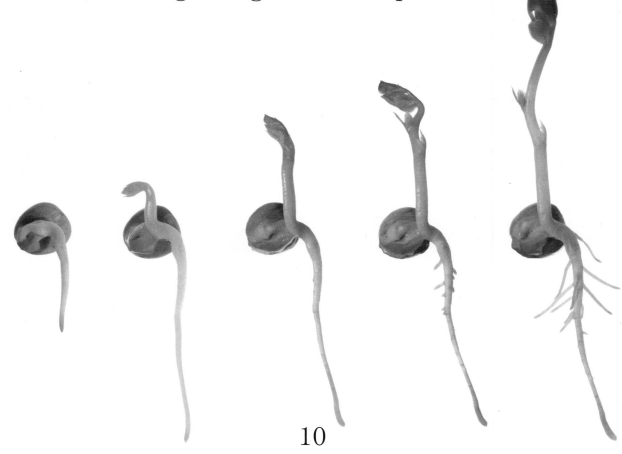

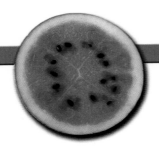

Root

Seed

A plant seed is much like a bird's egg. Inside the bird's egg are the beginnings of a new bird. Inside a plant seed are the beginnings of a new plant.

Seeds

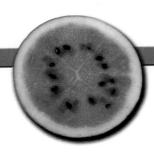

13

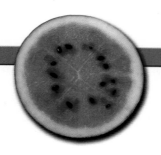

A plant seed holds food, too. The tiny plant in the seed uses that food to grow. Soon it grows new leaves. Then the new leaves make the plants food.

14

PARTS OF A PLANT

Leaves

Stem

Seed

Roots

15

Growing Seeds

A plant doesn't **hatch** like a chick from an egg. A plant **germinates**. That means the tiny plant breaks through the seed cover and begins to grow.

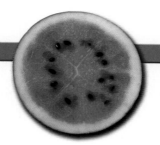

Seeds germinate when they have just the right amount of water, air, and temperature. A typical seed has two growth points. One grows a **stem**. The other grows roots.

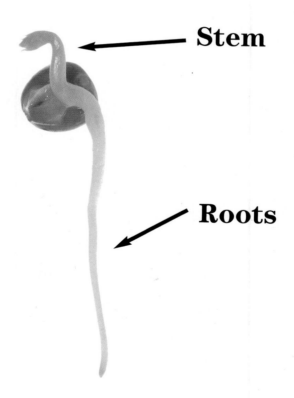

Stem

Roots

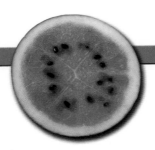

The wind can carry a seed a long way. Animals carry seeds, too. Some seeds stick to animal fur. Plants keep growing with every new seed.

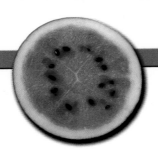

Glossary

coconut (KOH kuh nuht) — a very large nut with a hard shell

fruit (FROOT) — ripening seeds and their covering

germinate (JUR muh nate) — to start new plant life

hatch (HACH) — to break through an egg

orchid (OR kid) — a family of flowering plants that make tiny, dust-like seeds

stem (stem) — the part of the plant that the leaves, flowers, and fruit are attached to.

Index

Further Reading

Matthews, Rachel. *Seeds*. Chrysalis Education, 2006.

Wallace, Nancy. *Seeds! Seeds! Seeds!*. Marshall
   Cavendish, 2007.

Websites to Visit

www.kathimitchel.com/plants.html

www.picadome.fcps.net/lab/currl/plants/default.htm

About the Author

Lynn M. Stone is the author of more than 400 children's books. He is a talented natural history photographer as well. Lynn, a former teacher, travels worldwide to photograph wildlife in its natural habitat.